C000193481

1 MONTH OF
FREE
READING

at

www.ForgottenBooks.com

By purchasing this book you are eligible for one month membership to ForgottenBooks.com, giving you unlimited access to our entire collection of over 700,000 titles via our web site and mobile apps.

To claim your free month visit:
www.forgottenbooks.com/free438870

* Offer is valid for 45 days from date of purchase. Terms and conditions apply.

ISBN 978-0-483-78821-3
PIBN 10438870

This book is a reproduction of an important historical work. Forgotten Books uses
state-of-the-art technology to digitally reconstruct the work, preserving the original format
whilst repairing imperfections present in the aged copy. In rare cases, an imperfection in
the original, such as a blemish or missing page, may be replicated in our edition. We do,
however, repair the vast majority of imperfections successfully; any imperfections that
remain are intentionally left to preserve the state of such historical works.

Forgotten Books is a registered trademark of FB &c Ltd.
Copyright © 2017 FB &c Ltd.
FB &c Ltd, Dalton House, 60 Windsor Avenue, London, SW19 2RR.
Company number 08720141. Registered in England and Wales.

For support please visit www.forgottenbooks.com

EIGHTY-THIRD ANNUAL REPORT

OF THE

TRUSTEES

OF THE

PUBLIC LIBRARY

OF THE

CITY OF BOSTON

1934

BOSTON
PUBLISHED BY THE TRUSTEES
1936

6 201.5
1934

Boston Public Library
Sept. 29, 1936

THE PUBLIC LIBRARY OF THE CITY OF BOSTON· PRINTING DEPARTMENT

7.8.36. 2500

TRUSTEES OF THE PUBLIC LIBRARY

WILLIAM CARDINAL O'CONNELL, *President*
Term expires April 30, 1937

FRANK W. BUXTON
Term expires April 30, 1935

ELLERY SEDGWICK
Term expires April 30, 1938

JOHN L. HALL
Term expires April 30, 1936

LOUIS E. KIRSTEIN
Term expires April 30, 1939

MILTON E. LORD

DIRECTOR, AND LIBRARIAN

ORGANIZATION OF THE LIBRARY DEPARTMENT.

The Trustees of the Public Library of the City of Boston, organized in 1852, are now incorporated under the provisions of Chapter 114 of the Acts of 1878, as amended. The Board for 1852 was a preliminary organization; that for 1853 made the first annual report. The Board at present consists of five citizens at large, appointed by the Mayor for five-year terms, the term of one member expiring each year. The following citizens at large have been members of the Board since its organization in 1852:

ABBOTT, GORDON, A.B., 1926–1931.
ABBOTT, SAMUEL APPLETON BROWNE, A.M., 1879–95.
APPLETON THOMAS GOLD, A.M., 1852–56.
BENTON, JOSIAH HENRY, LL.D., 1894–1917.
BIGELOW, JOHN PRESCOTT, A.M., 1852–68.
BOWDITCH, HENRY INGERSOLL, M.D., 1865–67.
BOWDITCH, HENRY PICKERING, M.D., 1894–1902.
BOYLE, THOMAS FRANCIS, 1902–12.
BRAMAN, JARVIS DWIGHT, 1869–72.
BRETT, JOHN ANDREW, LL.B., 1912–16.
BUXTON, FRANK W., A.B., 1928–
CARR, SAMUEL, 1895–96, 1908–22.
CHASE, GEORGE BIGELOW, A.M., 1876–85.
CLARKE, JAMES FREEMAN, D.D., 1879–88.
COAKLEY, DANIEL HENRY, 1917–19.
CONNOLLY, ARTHUR THEODORE, 1916–1932.
CURRIER, GUY WILBUR, 1922–1930.
CURTIS, DANIEL SARGENT, A.M., 1873–75.
DE NORMANDIE, JAMES, D.D, 1895–1908.
DWIGHT, THOMAS, M.D., 1899–1908.
DWINNELL, CLIFTON HOWARD, B.S., 1927–28.
EVERETT, EDWARD, LL.D., 1852–64.
FROTHINGHAM, RICHARD, LL.D., 1875–79.
GASTON, WILLIAM ALEXANDER, LL.B., 1923–27.
GREEN, SAMUEL ABBOTT, M.D., 1868–78.
GREENOUGH, WILLIAM WHITWELL, 1856–88.
HALL, JOHN LOOMER, A.B., LL.B., 1931–
HAYNES, HENRY WILLIAMSON, A.M., 1880–94.
HILLIARD, GEORGE STILLMAN, LL.D., 1872–75;1876–77.
KENNEY, WILLIAM FRANCIS, A.M., 1908–1921.
KIRSTEIN, LOUIS EDWARD, 1919–
LEWIS, WESTON, 1868–79.
LEWIS, WINSLOW, M.D., 1867.
LINCOLN, SOLOMON, A.M., 1897–1907.
MANN, ALEXANDER, D.D., 1908–1923.
MORTON, ELLIS WESLEY, 1870–73.
MURRAY, MICHAEL JOSEPH, LL.B., 1921–26.
O'CONNELL, WILLIAM CARDINAL, 1932–

WALKER, FRANCIS AMASA, LL.D., 1896.
WHIPPLE, EDWIN PERCY, A.M., 1868–70.
WHITMORE, WILLIAM HENRY, A.M., 1885–88.
WINSOR, JUSTIN, LL.D., 1867–68.

The HON. EDWARD EVERETT was President of the Board from 1852 to 1864; GEORGE TICKNOR, in 1865; WILLIAM W. GREENOUGH, from 1866 to April, 1888; PROF. HENRY W. HAYNES, from May 7, 1888, to May 12, 1888; SAMUEL A. B. ABBOTT, May 12, 1888, to April 30, 1895; HON. F. O. PRINCE, October 8, 1895, to May 8, 1899; SOLOMON LINCOLN, May 12, 1899, to October 15, 1907; REV. JAMES DE NORMANDIE, January 31, 1908, to May 8, 1908; JOSIAH H. BENTON, May 8, 1908, to February 6, 1917; WILLIAM F. KENNEY, February 13, 1917, to May 7, 1920; REV. ALEXANDER MANN, May 7, 1920, to January 22, 1923; MSGR. ARTHUR T. CONNOLLY, April 13, 1923 to June 13, 1924; LOUIS E. KIRSTEIN, June 13, 1924 to June 19, 1925; HON. MICHAEL J. MURRAY, June 19, 1925 to July 2, 1926; GUY W. CURRIER, July 2, 1926 to May 2, 1927; MSGR. ARTHUR T. CONNOLLY, May 2, 1927 to June 22, 1928; LOUIS E. KIRSTEIN, June 22, 1928 to June 21, 1929; GORDON ABBOTT, June 21, 1929 to June 20, 1930; FRANK W. BUXTON, June 20, 1930 to May 15, 1931; LOUIS E. KIRSTEIN, May 15, 1931 to May 20, 1932; ELLERY SEDGWICK, May 20, 1932 to May 5, 1933; JOHN L. HALL, May 5, 1933 to May 18, 1934; WILLIAM CARDINAL O'CONNELL since May 18, 1934.

LIBRARIANS.

(From 1858 to 1877, the chief executive officer was called Superintendent; from 1923 to 1934 Director; since 1934 Director and Librarian.)

CAPEN, EDWARD, *Librarian*, May 13, 1852 – December 16, 1874.

JEWETT, CHARLES C., *Superintendent*, 1858 – January 9, 1868.

WINSOR, JUSTIN, LL.D., *Superintendent*, February 25, 1868 – September 30, 1877.

GREEN, SAMUEL A., M.D., *Trustee, Acting Librarian*, October 1, 1877 – September 30, 1878.

CHAMBERLAIN, MELLEN, LL.D, *Librarian*, October 1, 1878 – September 30, 1890.

DWIGHT, THEODORE F., *Librarian*, April 13, 1892 – April 30, 1894.

PUTNAM, HERBERT, LL.D., *Librarian*, February 11, 1895 – April 3, 1899.

WHITNEY, JAMES L., A.M., *Acting Librarian*, March 31, 1899 – December 21, 1899; *Librarian*, December 22, 1899 – January 31, 1903

WADLIN, HORACE G., LITT.D., *Librarian*, February 1, 1903 – March 15, 1917; *Acting Librarian*, March 15, 1917 – June 15, 1917.

BELDEN, CHARLES F. D., A.M., LL.B., LITT.D., *Director*, March 15, 1917 – October 24, 1931.

LORD, MILTON E., A.B., *Director, and Librarian*, since February 1, 1932.

LIBRARY SYSTEM, JANUARY 1, 1934

DEPARTMENTS.	¶OPENED.
*Central Library, Copley Square	May 2, 1854
*East Boston Branch, 276–282 Meridian St.	Jan. 28, 1871
§South Boston Branch, 372 West Broadway	May 1, 1872
‖Fellowes Athenæum Branch, 46 Millmont St.	July 16, 1873
*Charlestown Branch, 43 Monument Square	Jan. 5, 1874
*Brighton Branch, 40 Academy Hill Road	Jan. 5, 1874
‡Dorchester Branch, Arcadia, cor. Adams St.	Jan. 25, 1875
†Lower Mills Branch, 1110 Washington, cor. Richmond St. . .	June 7, 1875
‡South End Branch, 65 West Brookline St.	Aug., 1877
†Jamaica Plain Branch, 12 Sedgwick, cor. South St. . . .	June, 1876
‡Roslindale Branch, 4210 Washington St.	Dec. 3, 1878
*West Roxbury Branch, 1961 Centre St.	Jan. 6, 1880
*Mattapan Branch, 8–10 Hazleton St.	Dec. 27, 1881
*North End Branch, 3a North Bennet St.	Oct., 1882
§Neponset Branch, 362 Neponset Ave.	Jan. 1, 1883
§Mt. Bowdoin Branch, 275 Washington St.	Nov. 1, 1886
§Allston Branch, 161 Harvard Ave.	Mar. 11, 1889
‡Codman Square Branch, Washington, cor. Norfolk St. . .	Nov. 12, 1890
‡Mt. Pleasant Branch, 335 Dudley, cor Vine St.	Nov. 12, 1890
‡Tyler Street Branch, 130 Tyler, cor. Oak St.	Jan. 16, 1896
*West End Branch, 131 Cambridge St.	Feb. 1, 1896
‡Upham's Corner Branch, 500 Columbia Rd.	Mar. 16, 1896
‡Memorial Branch, cor. Warren and Townsend Sts. . .	May 1, 1896
§Roxbury Crossing Branch, 208 Ruggles, cor Tremont St. . .	Jan. 18, 1897
*Boylston Branch, 433 Centre St.	Nov. 1, 1897
§Orient Heights Branch, 5 Butler Ave.	June 25, 1901
‡City Point Branch, Municipal Bldg., Broadway	July 18, 1906
*Parker Hill Branch, 1497 Tremont St.	July 15, 1907
*Hyde Park Branch, 35 Harvard Ave., cor. Winthrop St. . .	Jan. 1, 1912
*Faneuil Branch, 419 Faneuil St.	Mar. 4, 1914
§Andrew Square Branch, 394 Dorchester St.	Mar. 5, 1914
*Jeffries Point Branch, 222 Webster St.	Oct. 15, 1921
‡Baker Library, Harvard Graduate School of Business Administration	Jan. 15, 1927
*Kirstein Memorial Library Building: 20 City Hall Ave. . .	May 7, 1930
Business Branch, first and second floors;	
Kirstein Branch, third floor.	
§Phillips Brooks Branch, 12 Hamilton St., Readville . . .	May 18, 1931

¶In the case of the Central Library and some of the branches the opening was in a different location from that now occupied. *In building owned by City and controlled by Library Board. †In building owned by City, and exclusively devoted to library uses. ‡In City building, in part devoted to other municipal uses. §Occupies rented rooms. ‖The lessee of the Fellowes Athenæum, a private library association. ‡Under agreement with Harvard.

CONTENTS

REPORT OF THE TRUSTEES 1

BALANCE SHEET 6

REPORT OF THE EXAMINING COMMITTEE 12

REPORT OF THE DIRECTOR 20

APPENDIX 27

To His Honor Frederick W. Mansfield,

Mayor of the City of Boston.

Sir:

The Trustees of the Public Library of the City of Boston present the following report of its condition and affairs for the year ending December 31, 1934, being the eighty-third annual report.

ORGANIZATION OF THE BOARD

The Corporation organized at the annual meeting on May 18, 1934 with the election of His Eminence William Cardinal O'Connell as President, Mr. Frank W. Buxton as Vice President, and Miss Elizabeth B. Brockunier as Clerk.

Mr. Louis E. Kirstein, whose term as a Trustee expired on April 30, was re-appointed for the term ending April 30, 1939.

BUDGET ESTIMATES

The estimates submitted on November 1, 1933 for the maintenance of the Library during the year 1934 were later amended and reduced. These estimates were as follows:

Item	Original estimate	Amount allowed
A.— Personal service	$805,850.56	$824,719.00
B.— Service other than personal	95,815.00	74,065.00
C.— Equipment	175,859.00	117,000.00
D.— Supplies	34,690.00	33,200.00
E.— Materials	22,450.00	21,000.00
H.— Emergency Relief Projects	30,000.00	36,425.81
Total	$1,164,664.56	$1,106,409.81

The amount allowed for Personal Service originally was $800,000. This was subsequently increased to $824,719 to permit in 1934 the resumption of step rate increases in pay discontinued since 1931. During 1934 there were also in effect salary reductions for all city employees on a graduated basis of 5%, 10%, and 15%.

RECEIPTS OF THE LIBRARY

The receipts which may be expended by the Trustees for the maintenance of the Library consist of the annual appropriation by the Mayor and City Council, and the income from Trust Funds given to the institution and invested by the City Treasurer. During the year 1934 these receipts were:

Annual appropriation	$1,106,409.81
Income from trust funds	26,306.01
Unexpended balance of trust funds income of previous years .	60,080.50
Total	$1,192,796.32

Receipts which were accounted for and paid into the City Treasury for general municipal purposes during the year were as follows:

From fines	$22,082.17
From sales of waste paper .	59.28
From sales of catalogs, etc. .	122.31
From commission on telephone stations	487.13
From payments for lost books	659.61
Refund	4.51
	$23,415.01

EXPENDITURES OF THE LIBRARY

The total amount expended during 1934 was $1,130,706.28 This was divided as follows:

From city appropriation .	$1,106,409.81
From deposits in London	1,205.85
From special appropriations .	6.80
From the income of trust funds	23,083.82

ADDITIONS TO THE LIBRARY

The number of volumes added to the Library during the year was 66,059, obtained chiefly by purchase, but in some part by gift and exchange. The total number of volumes in the Library at the close of the year was 1,673,609.

The total amount expended for books, periodicals, newspapers, photographs, and other library material from the city appropriation and from the trust funds income was $120,494.05.

USE OF THE LIBRARY

The home use of books for the year was 5,194,351. The use of material within the Library's premises for reference and study is for the most part unrestricted, and it is therefore impracticable to record it.

In addition to the above noted use of the Central Library and the thirty-four Branch Libraries, deposits of books were made available to 321 agencies, including engine houses, institutions, and schools.

COMPARATIVE STATISTICS, 1933 and 1934

A comparison of certain statistics of 1934 with those for 1933 is noted below:

	1933	1934
Total expenditures: city appropriation and trust funds income	$1,034,945.75	$1,130,699.48
Expended for books and other library material from city appropriation and trust funds income	119,076.63	120,494.05
Number of Volumes added	68,175	66,059
Total number of volumes in the Library	1,654,017	1,673,609
Borrowed for home use	5,548,283	5,194,351
Number of card holders	197,458	182,470

RE-ORGANIZATION OF THE LIBRARY

Steps were taken during the year to effect additional development of the revised plan of organization of the Library adopted by the Board in September 1932. A detailed statement of these steps is included in the report of the Director, to be found on pages 20–26 below.

BUILDINGS AND EQUIPMENT

Constant vigilance has been necessary in the matter of the level of the ground water in the vicinity of the Central Library building. Close attention has been given to its study, particularly as it affects the underpinning, the foundations, and the superstructure of the building.

The emergency relief activities of the Federal Government under its Civil Works Administration made possible extensive painting of walls and floors both at the Central Library and in the Branch Libraries. A large project was also carried on under these auspices for the cleaning of books throughout the entire library system.

FEDERAL EMERGENCY RELIEF PROJECTS CARRIED ON UNDER THE DIRECTION OF THE LIBRARY

In addition to the above physical improvements effected as part of the emergency relief projects of the Federal Government there were carried on two additional large projects, first under the Civil Works Administration, and subsequently under the Federal Emergency Relief Administration. The first of these provided for changing the cards in the several card catalogs of the Central Library to the uniform size employed in most American libraries. The second provided for the changing of the shelf lists of the Central Library from their old handwritten folio volumes to a modern arrangement on uniform size catalog cards. Both of these projects have contributed materially to making possible an eventual development along modern lines of certain of the Library's processes in which improvement has long been desired. The latter project is continuing into the coming year.

Approximately seven hundred individuals have been employed, their wages being provided by the Federal Government, and special provision for incidental expenses being made by the City.

GIFTS

During the year the Library received many important gifts of books and other library material. A list of the principal gifts is to be found in the Appendix on pages 35–37.

TRUST FUNDS

The Trustees welcome bequests of money and hope that generous testators may remember the Library. It is from such sources only that they can make purchases of rare and other important books that give value and prestige to a great educational institution such as the Library has become.

As a matter of interest to the public the Board has pleasure in listing herein the present trust funds of the Library, with explanatory notes. The list will be found on pages 38–48 below.

EXAMINING COMMITTEE

The Trustees gratefully acknowledge the assistance given by the Examining Committee of 1934. Its membership included the following individuals:

Hon. Elijah Adlow
Mr. George Bramwell Baker
Mr. Walter B. Briggs
Dr. Arthur H. Cole
Mr. Ralph Adams Cram
Hon. James M. Curley
Miss Susan J. Ginn
Mr. Francis X. Hurley
Dr. Henry Jackson
Mr. Herbert F. Jenkins
Mr. Henry Lewis Johnson
Mr. Carl T. Keller
Rev. Robert H. Lord
Mr. Charles D. Maginnis

Mr. George R. Nutter
Hon. James P. Parmenter
Mrs. Elizabeth W. Perkins
Mrs. Edward M. Pickman
Hon. Abraham E. Pinanski
Mr. Robert Proctor
Mr. Charles M. Rogerson
Mrs. Arthur A. Shurcliff
Mrs. Francis E. Slattery
Rev. William M. Stinson
Mr. Charles H. Taylor
Mr. D. B. Updike
Dr. Henry R. Viets
Mr. Charles F. Weed

Mrs. Frederick Winslow

It is gratifying to have the generous and helpful assistance of citizens who render such service. Special attention is called to the constructive report of the Committee as it appears on pages 12–19, immediately following.

CONCLUSION

Attention is called to the report of the Director of the Library as found on pages 20–26 below. It presents the important developments within the Library during the course of the year.

To the entire Library staff we wish here to express our appreciation of the work which they have rendered to the public.

FRANK W. BUXTON
JOHN L. HALL
LOUIS E. KIRSTEIN
WILLIAM CARDINAL O'CONNELL
ELLERY SEDGWICK

BALANCE SHEET, RECEIPTS AND

Dr.]

Central Library and Branches:
  To Expenditures For
    Permanent employees (exclusive of Printing
      and Binding employees) $637,626.02
    Temporary employees 116,152.06
                                                      ——————— $753,778 08

  To Service Other Than Personal
    Printing and binding 61.04
    Advertising 2.50
    Transportation of persons 1,808.03
    Cartage and freight 7,108.01
    Light and power 21,203.77
    Rent, taxes and water 18,112.74
    Surety, bond and insurance 389.25
    Communication 4,049.23
    Cleaning 1,002.71
    Removal of ashes 13.60
    Removal of snow 363.10
    Medical 2.00
    Expert 1,853.48
    Fees 20.00
    Photographic and blueprinting 125.30
    General plant 25,495.71
                                                      ——————— 81,610.47

  To Expenditure for Equipment
    Machinery 1,571.58
    Motorless vehicles 23.00
    Furniture and fittings 4,617.76
    Office 1,473.07
    Books:
      City appropriation   85,195.67
      Trust funds income
        (including transfer to
        London account)   17,841.23   103,036.90
    Newspapers:
      City appropriation   918.18
      Trust funds income   1,715.25   2,633.43
    Music:
      City appropriation   77.06
      Trust funds income   1,108.87   1,185.93
    Lantern slides:
      Trust funds income   31.25
    Periodicals:
      City appropriation   13,183.72
      Trust funds income   286.22   13,469.94
    Photographs:
      City appropriation   45.00
      Trust funds income   91.60   136.60
    Tools and instruments 975.67
    General Plant 770.46
                                                      ———————
                                                         99 5 59

EXPENSES, DECEMBER 31, 1934

Cr.

By City Appropriation 1934 . . . . .$1,106,409.81
By Income from Trust Funds 26,306.01
By Income from J. L. Whitney
    Bibliographic Account 700.00
By Transfer from Domestic Funds to
    London Account 4,000.00
                                         1,137,415.82

Carried forward $1,137,415.82

2

BALANCE SHEET, RECEIPTS AND

DR.

Brought forward		$965,314.14
To EXPENDITURES FOR SUPPLIES		
Office	7,992.84	
Food	15.30	
Fuel	20,169.73	
Forage and animal	16.70	
Medical	36.97	
Laundry, cleaning, toilet	1,965.61	
Agricultural	356.39	
Chemicals and disinfectants	258.08	
General plant	2,571.67	
		33,383.29
To EXPENDITURES FOR MATERIAL		
Building	5,080.03	
Electrical	3,778.05	
General plant	1,483.82	
		10,341.90
To EXPENDITURES FOR F.E.R.A. PROJECTS		41,042.37
To SPECIAL ITEMS		
J. L. Whitney Bibliographic account		2,087.25
To BINDING DEPARTMENT:		
Salaries	55,530.39	
Light	55.26	
Repairs	265.36	
Equipment	216.39	
Supplies	9.37	
Building material	1.30	
Stock	5,816.11	
		61,894.18
To PRINTING DEPARTMENT:		
Salaries	12,666.04	
Light	47.54	
Communication	3.78	
Repairs	912.65	
Equipment	663.64	
Supplies	38.96	
Stock	2,162.45	
Outside work	141.29	
		16,636.35
To SPECIAL APPROPRIATION:		
Branch Libraries, Establishment of		6.80
To AMOUNT PAID INTO CITY TREASURY:		
Fines	22,082.17	
Sales of catalogues, bulletins	122.31	
Commission on telephone stations	487.13	
Payments for lost books	659.61	
Refunds	4.51	
Sales of waste paper	59.28	
		23,415.01

EXPENSES, DECEMBER 31, 1934

CR.

Brought forward	$1,137,415.82
BY BALANCE BROUGHT FORWARD FROM 1933:	
Trust funds income, City Treasury	60,080.50
Trust funds income, on deposit in London . .	40.88
City appropriation on deposit in London . . .	1,528.89
James L. Whitney Bibliographic account . . .	4,161.98
Library Building, Fireproofing, improvements, etc. .	16,524.80
Library Building, Foundations	19,747.96
Branch Libraries, Establishment of	7,309.80
H. C. Bentley Gift	220.38
	109,615.19

Carried forward $1,247,031.01

BALANCE SHEET, RECEIPTS AND

Dr.

Brought forward		$1,154,121.29
To Balance, December 31, 1934:		
Trust funds income on deposit in London . .	1,901.57	
City appropriation on deposit in London . . .	323.04	
Trust Funds income, City Treasury	67,529.25	
James L. Whitney Bibliographic account . . .	2,774.73	
H. C. Bentley Gift	220.38	
		72,748.97
To Balance Unexpended, December 31, 1934:		
Central Library Building, Fireproofing . . .	16,524.80	
Central Library Building, Foundation . . .	19,747.96	
Branch Libraries, Establishment of	7,303.00	
		43,575.76

Carried forward	$1,270,446.02

EXPENSES, DECEMBER 31, 1934

C<small>R.</small>

Brought forward	$1,247,031.01
B<small>Y</small> R<small>ECEIPTS</small>:	
From Fines	22,082.17
Sales of catalogues, bulletins and lists . . .	122.31
Commissions on telephone stations	487.13
Payments for lost books	659.61
Refunds	4.51
Sales of waste paper	59.28
	23,415.01

$1,270,446.02

REPORT OF THE EXAMINING COMMITTEE

To The Trustees of the Public Library
of the City of Boston.

Gentlemen:

The Examining Committee for the year 1934 respectfully submits its report.

ORGANIZATION OF THE COMMITTEE

In accordance with the recommendation made by the Committee of 1932, and pursued by the Committee of 1933, the Examining Committee of 1934 was appointed and met for organization in June. This gave opportunity for an adequate period of study and investigation and has made possible the rendering of its report within the limits of the calendar year. The several sub-committees assigned to the various divisions of the work have given careful consideration to the problems of the Library and in addition have visited the thirty-three branch libraries as a committee of the whole. Each member of the Committee visited three branches and only two members were assigned in most cases to each branch. As the complete findings of the various sub-committees are on file with the Library, it appears that a summary of the prominent features will suffice for this report.

BUILDINGS AND EQUIPMENT

Perhaps the question of buildings and equipment should have first attention. For some years there has been felt some concern relative to the foundations of the Central Library building. The life and strength of the foundations depend upon the preservation of the wooden piles upon which the building rests. The continuous checking and rechecking and recording of the water level in the ground under the Main Library building in Copley Square is of vital importance and should be continued. There seems also to be a pressing need for decreasing floor loads, especially in the bookstacks. This leads the Committee to endorse the plans being developed by the Director for rearrangements in the use of space in the Central Library building, with a view to bringing about at the same time greater efficiency in administration. In addition to this the Committee hopes that the time will soon come to resume the policy of replacing existing inadequate branch library buildings in accordance with the long-time plan that was in force before the depression.

BOOK SELECTION

Next in importance is the consideration of the problem of the selection of books. Succeeding Committees have been faced constantly with the question of whether or not the Library has been maintaining a proper balance in its two main functions, namely, that of meeting popular library needs, and that of providing for scholarly reference needs. With limited funds it is obviously difficult to maintain a perfect balance in the fulfillment of these functions. Attempts should be made constantly to determine the proper ratio between investments in popular and scholarly material. The Committee of 1932 recommended that means be provided to enable the Library to make a survey of the demands for the various types of material and the sources of these demands, and to keep track continuously of the funds invested in books of various classes and various subject matters. A long step has been taken in this direction in the past year by the installation of tabulating machines, making possible the continuous collection of data as to the expenditures by groups, and the sources of the demand for the purchase of particular materials. The statistics thus obtained will be of aid to the library administration in determining with greater accuracy whether the Library's funds are being expended to meet the above needs in the best possible manner.

Last year's Committee called attention in its report to the improvement in the arrangements for book selection that has been brought about through the reorganization of the Library. It is hoped that as a result of this formal recognition of the function of book selection there will follow the appointment of expert personnel who will be conversant with the subjects with which the Library must deal. It is recognized, however, that there is a limit to the number of expert personnel who may be employed, and therefore it is recommended that those responsible for book selection have the benefit of recommendations from outside experts in their respective fields. The Committee suggests the possibility of securing the uncompensated assistance of qualified individuals who will be willing to aid in book selection. Such arrangements, no doubt, will result in a more useful development of the Library's collections, particularly for research purposes. Perhaps in this connection it is well to recommend also a thorough study of the collections in terms of their long-time development.

BOOKBINDING

Apparently facilities for bookbinding are at present inadequate to the needs of the Library. This, of necessity, brings about arrears in the repair and conditioning of books. As the use and the growth of the Library increase, this is likely to become a serious problem. The availability of Federal Emergency Relief Administration funds for aid in this direction is suggested for consideration. The problem of the conditioning of bindings is highly important, particularly in respect to the rare book collections. It is understood that the library administration is giving this problem serious study. Also it is noted that there are apparently differences of opinion as to the best methods for the preservation of valuable bindings. The Committee urges that this study be prosecuted without undue delay and that action follow upon the results at the earliest possible moment.

CATALOGING AND CLASSIFICATION

Funds made available by the Federal Emergency Relief Administration have enabled the Library to make extraordinary progress with some of the problems of its cataloging. Many problems which were apparent a year ago have been solved with the aid of these funds. As a result the Library will shortly be in a position to proceed to a reclassification of its collections along modern lines.

SPACE IN CENTRAL LIBRARY BUILDING

One of the problems of the Library that is rapidly becoming acute is that of finding space for its growing collections. Fundamental moves to meet this situation will apparently have to be taken during the coming year. In connection with the re-allocation of library space that may have to be considered, particularly in the Central Library, the Committee believes that certain general principles should be emphasized:

1. that the more accessible areas of the Library be employed for service to the public rather than for internal library administration;
2. that special collections of allied interest be brought into as close physical proximity as possible;
3. that the unsatisfactory conditions surrounding the location of the Statistical Department be eliminated;
4. that those portions of the Library at present employed for allied rather than purely library activities be converted in their use to purposes that are purely of a library nature, and in the Central Library more particularly for the adequate housing of the special collections.

It is a pleasure to learn that a beginning of this work of re-allocating space in the Central Library building can perhaps be made during the year that is ahead. In connection with this the Committee wishes to urge also that definite consideration be given to the problem of proper air conditioning throughout the Central Library building, and particularly in the Rare Book Department.

PUBLICATIONS

The question of the Library's publications is a vital one. The Committee wishes to suggest that the scholarly articles that have been appearing in the Library's monthly bulletin might be presented in a form more worthy of the dignity of a great scholarly library, perhaps in a quarterly publication designed for scholars, while the present monthly bulletin, or an adaptation thereof, might be continued under the title "More Books" and be developed for popular consumption, primarily through the branch libraries. The Committee believes that there is need for a popular bulletin as well as for a more dignified presentation of the Library's scholarly activities.

USE OF THE LIBRARY

A number of the problems met by the ordinary reader in his use of the Library were considered by a new sub-committee appointed for the first time this year, namely, that on the Use of the Library. It was the unanimous opinion of this sub-committee that improved service to the individual reader is the best possible way of encouraging the use of the Library. In this connection the Committee is particularly glad to learn of the plans under development by the Director for the establishment of a central administrative headquarters for readers in the Abbey Room, adjacent to the Issue Department and to the Bates Hall Card Catalogue and Reading Room, for the handling of complaints, the clearing up of misunderstandings, and the directing of readers, to the end that patrons of the Library may have full opportunity for satisfaction in their attempts to master the complexities of a large library system. The Committee offers also the suggestion that there be established a "waiting list" for books in constant demand, so that individual readers may be notified by postal card when in their turn these books become available for their use. It is recommended also that the many entrances and exits to the book stacks in the Central Library be reduced in number, so that unauthorized individuals may not have access to them; thus helping to reduce book losses from the shelves and also facilitating the checking of the work of the pages engaged in "running" for books requested by readers.

RELATIONSHIP OF THE LIBRARY TO SCHOOLS AND COLLEGES

The relationship of the Library to the schools and colleges of the city constitutes a vital problem. Good results have already been achieved in this direction. The Committee believes nevertheless that there are possibilities for developing a better relationship between the School Department and the Library Department through the establishment of a continuing committee to promote mutual understanding of the possibilities and limitations of each department's work. Much study can profitably be given to the entire question of this relationship of the Library to schools and colleges, particularly with reference to what the Library may reasonably be expected to contribute to the work of these institutions. The Committee fears that there is grave danger that colleges in the neighborhood of the Central Library look upon the Library as an annex to their own institutions.

BRANCH LIBRARIES

As noted at the beginning of this report each member of the Committee visited three branch libraries. In order that the members might conduct their visits intelligently and know exactly what they were expected to examine, eleven topics for investigation were agreed upon as covering the general condition of the branch libraries. These were as follows:

1. Is the entrance convenient and well lighted?
   Are there outside signs? Is the street outside well lighted at night?
2. Is the floor covering in good condition? Does it deaden the noise of footsteps?
3. Is the ventilation good? If not, how can it be improved?
4. Is the lighting good for readers? If not, can the position of the lights be changed, or can they be made brighter and more numerous without great expense?
5. Are adults and children so separated that adults have quiet?
6. Are the rooms overcrowded? If so, can this situation be relieved by re-arranging departments?
7. Where more than one floor is occupied, is there quick communication between floors, i.e., by speaking-tube or telephone?
8. Are the premises used for other than library purposes, to the detriment of the Library?
9. How is the staff accommodated as to work-rooms, typewriting space and rest-rooms?
10. Are there any special activities in the branch, i.e., collections of photographs, etc.?
11. Can any small improvements be made without much expense which will facilitate the work of the branch?

In addition to the answers to these questions, several recommendations were offered, all of which are included in the report of the Sub-Committee on Branch Libraries, on file with the Library. An additional point of interest is that of rendering the branch libraries less institutional in character. The Committee believes that this process might be aided in large measure through the formation of local committees, each committee being designed to take an interest in, and to support, the branch library of its own community.

FINANCE

The Committee has found in 1934 much the same conditions existing as in 1932 and in 1933 with respect to financial support. In those earlier years it seemed best, in view of the depression, not to set forth projects which, while needful, required increased expenditure, but to confine recommendations to the few matters which seemed fundamental. For instance, the Committees of each of the last two years recorded themselves strongly in favor of at least maintaining the service of the Library, and, if possible, expanding it; certainly not contracting it. It has been truly said that "the rediscovery of the Public Library is a by-product of the depression." This year's Committee wishes therefore earnestly to renew the recommendations made in the past two years, that the facilities of the Library be at least maintained, if not increased; and certainly not contracted.

It is the desire of this Committee that it be recorded as supporting the important recommendations of its predecessors. It hopes, for instance, that there may be carried out in the course of time the recommendation that there be established a body to be known as "The Friends of the Boston Public Library," from among whose members there might be furnished each year contributions, small or large, for the purchase of books and manuscripts which can not ordinarily be obtained through the Library's usual appropriations. Attention ought also to be given to plans for making better known to the public at large the substantial quantity of rare and valuable material in the possession of the Boston Public Library. Toward this end it is recommended that careful consideration be afforded to the publishing of a brochure presenting a brief history of the Library, enumerating its resources, listing its special collections, and pointing out the need for endowment to develop and build up these collections. Such a brochure ought to be the best specimen of the printer's art and have attractive illustrations. It should be made available to selected individuals, with the hope that they might thereby become interested in the Library and in the development of the Library's collections.

CONCLUSION

In conclusion the Committee wishes to state that it would be remiss in its duties if it did not pay tribute to the admirable work that is being done by the Director and his large corps of assistants. The desire of the Committee in offering its suggestions is simply to aid them in augmenting the good work already done.

Adopted as the Report of the Examining Committee, December 17, 1934.

Susan J. Ginn, *Vice Chairman*

Elijah Adlow
George Bramwell Baker
Walter B. Briggs
Walter S. Bucklin
Arthur H. Cole
Ralph Adams Cram
James M. Curley
Francis X. Hurley
Henry Jackson
Herbert F. Jenkins
Henry Lewis Johnson
Carl T. Keller
Robert H. Lord
Charles D. Maginnis

George R. Nutter
James P. Parmenter
Elizabeth W. Perkins
Hester Pickman
Abraham E. Pinanski
Robert Proctor
Charles M. Rogerson
Margaret M. Shurcliff
Lillian C. Slattery
William M. Stinson, S.J.
Charles H. Taylor
Henry R. Viets
Charles F. Weed
Mary W. Winslow

REPORT OF THE DIRECTOR

To the Trustees of the Public Library
of the City of Boston:

I submit herewith the report of the Director of the Library for the year ending December 31, 1934.

EFFECTS OF THE DEPRESSION

The economic depression continued to be clearly recognizable in its effects upon the Library's work throughout the year. The increased use of books and facilities that had begun after 1929 was sustained in appreciable fashion, though not quite to the same high degree as in 1932 and 1933. Appropriations for the support of the Library remained perceptibly depressed; even though their total for 1934 showed an increase over that for 1933, they were notably below the level that had prevailed for a considerable period preceding 1933.

Increased demands were made upon the Library in sponsoring and carrying out work projects for the relief of the unemployed, under the auspices of the Federal Emergency Relief Administration.

CONTINUING INCREASED USE OF THE LIBRARY

The experience of the year indicated that the increased use of books arising out of the depression conditions prevailing since 1929 was being sustained in appreciable fashion. During 1934 there were borrowed for home reading 5,194,351 volumes. This figure represents a 32% increase over that for 1929.

The following table shows the greatly increased use of the Library during five years of economic depression, 1930 – 1934:

	NO. OF BOOKS LENT FOR HOME USE	PERCENTAGE OF INCREASE OR DECREASE OVER PRECEDING YEAR	PERCENTAGE OF INCREASE OVER 1929
1929	3,930,068		
1930	4,133,459	+ 5%	+ 5%
1931	4,702,932	+13%	+20%
1932	5,567,681	+18%	+42%
1933	5,548,283	-0.3%	+41%
1934	5,194,351	- 6%	+32%

It is to be noted that in 1934 there occurred the first appreciable change in the trend of increase that had been prevailing since 1929. The number of books lent for home use in 1934 declined by 6% from the number lent in 1933. The average percentage of decrease during 1934 for the public libraries of the country at large was 8%.

There would seem to be two reasons underlying this change in 1934 from the trend of increase in existence from 1929 to 1933. The one — which is encouraging from a general point of view — is that improvement in general economic conditions has apparently been setting in; the unemployed are beginning to find employment once more, and there are therefore perhaps fewer of them to use libraries. The other — which is markedly discouraging from the particular point of view of the Library — is that the Library's books have become so worn out by the heavy use of the past four to five years that it is no longer possible to offer, them in sufficient quantity to meet the demand that nevertheless exists for them. It is to this latter situation that most weight is probably to be attached in indicating reasons for the decline in the number of books being borrowed.

In any case it is clear that the Library finished the year 1934 lending 32% more books than in 1929, the last of the pre-depression years. This is in itself an increase which is notable, despite its being slightly under the peak increases of 1932 and 1933.

APPROPRIATIONS FOR THE SUPPORT OF THE LIBRARY

The City appropriated for the support of the Library during 1934 the sum of $1,106,409.81. This was $101,659.81 greater than the amount appropriated in 1933. The increase was made up of the following items:

For miscellaneous needs	$15,515.00
For the resumption of step rate increases in pay	24,719.00
For the purchase of books	25,000.00
For emergency relief projects	36,425.81
	$101,659.81

Throughout many subdivisions of the budget it was necessary to make provision for rising costs of materials. For this purpose the additional appropriation of $15,515 was made.

With the advent of a new city administration in 1934 there was resumed the practice of granting step rate increases in pay for those groups of city workers who had been employed on such a basis prior to the discontinuance of the practice in 1931. The library employees had been such a group; consequently an additional appropriation in the amount of $24,719 was made for the purpose in the course of the year. The resumption of such step rate increases proved a most heartening measure to members of the library staff. It made possible also an adjustment in part of a number of cases in which inequalities had arisen through the discontinuance of the practice three years earlier.

The appropriation for the purchase of books had suffered severely when its amount had been dropped from $160,000 in 1932 to $75,000 in 1933. For 1934 the appropriation as first determined was set at $75,000; in the course of the year an additional amount of $25,000 was made available, in recognition of the need for books made acute by the heavily increased use of the Library arising out of the conditions of the economic depression. This additional appropriation proved of great aid. As shown above, the Library's books have been experiencing notably heavy use during the past five years. In fact they have been in process of being worn out at so great a rate that it is no longer possible to supply them in sufficient quantity, or in sufficiently good condition, to meet the public demands. The result has been that in 1934 there occurred a decline of 6% in the number of books borrowed by readers for home use, the first appreciable change in the trend of increase prevailing since 1929. There is little evidence that the demand for books on the part of the public has decreased notably. The chief reason for the decline is believed to be the depletion of the Library's book stock. Books are being worn out faster than they can be replaced. An acute situation in this respect is developing for the years immediately ahead.

For emergency relief projects a special appropriation was made in the amount of $36,425.81. This was for the purchase of supplies and materials and for the rental of space and equipment necessary for carrying on several extensive relief projects for which the cost of personnel was provided by the federal government.

UNEMPLOYMENT RELIEF PROJECTS

In the last weeks of 1933 the Library was asked to assume its share, together with other departments of the city government, in planning, sponsoring, and carrying out work projects for the unemployed, under the general auspices of the Civil Works Administration then being established by the federal government. Projects were initiated promptly and were continued from 1933 into 1934. Originally designed to be of ten weeks duration only, the projects were extended in length, and additional projects developed, under the auspices of the Federal Emergency Relief Administration in succession to the Civil Works Administration.

In the course of the year there was completed the work of the large C.W.A. project initiated to make possible the changing of the cards in the catalogues of the central library to the uniform size employed in most American libraries. This was succeeded by an F.E.R.A. project for changing the shelf lists of the central library from large bound folio volumes to uniform size catalogue cards. Other projects were carried on for the cleaning of books and for the painting of walls, floors, and the like throughout the library system.

These projects provided work for three to four hundred individuals in the course of the year. The cost of personnel was borne by the federal government as part of its program for the relief of the unemployed. The contribution on the part of the Library was that of directing the work, together with providing supplies and materials and renting space and equipment, for which purpose a special appropriation was made by the City.

FURTHER DEVELOPMENT OF
REORGANIZATION OF THE LIBRARY

During 1933 there was instituted a revised plan of organization for the Library which provided for the distribution of its activities between a Circulation Division (primarily the branch libraries), a Reference Division (primarily the central library), and a Division of Business Operations (for the business management of the entire library system). At the time fiscal conditions did not permit the appointment of officers to head either the Circulation Division or the Reference Division. It was possible, however, to make appointments to certain intermediate positions within the divisions.

In 1934 it became possible to proceed further. Appointments were made to the positions of Chief Librarian of the Circulation Division and Chief Librarian of the Reference Division. These officers, and the Comptroller at the head of the Division of Business Operations, are to be responsible for the entire functioning of their respective divisions. As division heads they are to report directly to the Director. They will be the second ranking officers of the Library. The Director is thus to become the general administrator of the entire library system, with the division heads serving as the active executive officers of the respective divisions.

One other major change was made during the year. In the Reference Division recognition was given to the importance of the extensive rare book collections in the possession of the Library, and their need for special attention, through the establishment of the position of Keeper of Rare Books.

Further developments in the reorganization of the Library will be necessary as conditions permit. For the moment certain limitations, primarily in physical facilities, prevent the complete realization of many desirable rearrangements of departmental relationships, particularly along functional lines. Attempts to achieve these will have to be made from time to time. A library is an organic body. It must recognize that evolution and change are a necessary part of its lot.

TRAINING OF PERSONNEL

In 1933 there was instituted an extensive and wide program of training courses open to all full-time members of the library staff. This program was put into full effect at the beginning of the academic year in October 1933.

During the academic year 1933–34 there were 261 members of the library staff enrolled in twelve full courses (three terms of ten weeks each) and nine one-term courses. Of these individuals 202 completed the work satisfactorily; 71 did so with distinction.

The academic year 1934–35 found 168 members of the staff enrolled for courses beginning with the autumn term. Additional enrollments were indicated for the one-term courses to follow in the winter and spring terms.

Enrollment in the courses is voluntary. The individual has to undertake the work in his own, not library, time. The courses are conceived primarily as a sharing of experience, knowledge, and thought by the more advanced members of the staff with those less advanced.

These training courses are not expected to produce results that will necessarily be extraordinary. They will have been worth while if they afford an opportunity for training to those who feel in need thereof but have not previously had such a possibility within their reach, or if they afford supplementary work for those who have had formal library training elsewhere. For the Library there should eventually follow a raising of the level of the qualifications of the staff as a whole. It is of no little significance that two hundred members of the library staff are engaged in work and study in such courses.

PERSONNEL CHANGES

The following appointments to titular positions were made during the year: Orlando C. Davis, as Chief Librarian of the Circulation Division; Richard G. Hensley, as Acting Chief Librarian of the Reference Division; James W. Kenney, as Acting Comptroller; Zoltán Haraszti, as Keeper of Rare

Books; and Francis J. Hannigan, as Supervisor of Special Reference Departments.

Under the provisions of the Boston Retirement Act the following individuals retired from the library service: Emil L. Hofman, Pressman in the Printing Department, after 24 years service; and Mary A. Hopkins, Cleaner, after 23 years service.

By death the Library lost the services of Cecilia W. Kueffner, Cataloger in the Cataloging and Classification Department, and Helen R. Needham, Second Assistant in the Boylston Branch Library.

CONCLUSION

Attention is called to the statistical summaries that appear in the Appendix to this Report.

The Director has pleasure in acknowledging constant support from Trustees and Library Staff alike. It has meant much to the work of the Library.

Respectfully submitted,
MILTON E. LORD
Director, and Librarian

APPENDIX

TABLES OF CENTRAL AND BRANCH CIRCULATION

	1929	1930	1931	1932	1933	1934
Central Library	676,240	698,627	728,656	777,666	793,121	756,018
Business Branch		6,157*	13,193	16,604	17,614	18,410
Allston	97,445	108,557	137,709	175,054	192,331	186,413
Andrew Square	110,225	116,196	128,337	155,574	145,801	138,638
Boylston	80,097	79,946	94,306	147,862	143,764	138,595
Brighton	92,223	103,145	121,032	139,276	147,666	134,388
Charlestown	100,483	100,914	119,637	136,845	144,676	127,866
City Point	83,558	97,264	122,619	155,492	150,036	144,762
Codman Square	153,372	158,881	186,386	216,780	199,786	185,451
Dorchester	99,255	102,790	115,810	137,018	140,344	132,104
East Boston	145,759	157,746	180,859	218,072	214,789	188,819
Faneuil	72,005	78,436	90,424	120,007	130,252	138,234
Fellowes Athen.	88,381	85,739	93,970	114,937	109,077	98,118
Hyde Park	108,512	120,878	127,888	154,838	149,875	144,011
Jamaica Plain	85,935	95,895	118,561	133,335	131,903	126,702
Jeffries Point	62,111	70,768	75,459	100,736	92,499	80,460
Kirstein		18,020*	43,196	56,971	65,149	63,388
Lower Mills	44,730	52,279	59,692	76,137	81,017	74,990
Mattapan	133,210	139,723	187,669	220,675	219,300	205,498
Memorial	180,344	178,467	213,320	246,739	246,757	222,975
Mt. Bowdoin	134.008	134,310	151,456	168,036	158,667	149,341
Mt. Pleasant	72,167	76,956	82,795	100,361	102,914	94,640
Neponset	51,228	57,043	60,986	75,148	78,579	69,638
North End	145,201	145,326	158,333	185,849	163,735	143,351
Orient Heights	42,571	56,954	60,512	84,887	84,233	92,801
Parker Hill	56,209	60,815	112,308	130,042	125,524	119,139
Phillips Brooks		.	25,713*	50,383	51,870	46,258
Roslindale	124,995	130,268	151,956	170,287	173,078	167,562
Roxbury Crossnig	78,803	80,022	69,034	77,650	76,023	75,062
South Boston	171,805	163,266	161,244	189,904	168,326	141,046
South End	123,794	124,352	122,870	150,745	155,575	154,604
Tyler Street	46,058	51,195	59,163	74,230	72,334	52,578
Uphams Corner	169,027	184,595	201,701	225,285	228,490	211,399
West End	180,854	177,125	189,543	219,413	218,721	208,003
West Roxbury	119,463	120,804	136,595	164,843	174,457	163,089
Total	3,930,068	4,133,459	4,702,932	5,567,681	5,548,283	5,194,351

*For eight months, May through December.

The net gains and losses in circulation are presented, apart from the totals, in the following form:

		VOLUMES
1929 gain over preceding year	. . . .	30,782
1930 gain over preceding year	. . . .	203,391
1931 gain over preceding year	. . . .	569,473
1932 gain over preceding year	. . . .	864,749
1933 loss from preceding year	. . . .	19,398
1934 loss from preceding year	. . . .	353,932

USE OF BOOKS

CIRCULATION FROM CENTRAL BY MONTHS

	HOME USE DIRECT	BRANCH DEPT. HOME USE THROUGH	SCHOOLS AND INSTITUTIONS THROUGH BRANCH DEPT.	TOTALS
January 1934 . .	37,716	7,958	33,760	79,434
Februray " . .	34,885	6,997	35,186	77,068
March " . .	39,554	8,331	35,436	83,321
April " . .	35,638	6,430	35,838	77,906
May " . .	32,208	6,141	37,112	75,461
June " . .	24,849	4,851	14,433	44,133
July " . .	25,582	4,622	4,584	34,788
August " . .	25,408	4,894	4,193	34,495
September " . .	28,923	5,291	2,995	37,209
October " . .	38,245	7,800	16,215	62,260
November " . .	37,822	7,770	28,248	73,840
December " . .	34,610	7,033	34,460	76,103
Totals . .	395,440	78,118	282,460	756,018

DISTRIBUTION OF TOTAL CIRCULATION

CENTRAL LIBRARY:	HOME USE	SCHOOLS AND INSTITUTIONS	TOTALS
a. Direct	395,440		
b. Through Branches			
1. Deposit Collections . . .	51,672		
2. General Collections . . .	26,446		
c. Schools and Institutions through Branch Department . . .		282,460	756,018
BUSINESS BRANCH			18,410
BRANCHES:			
Allston	186,413	. . . .	186,413
Andrew Square	138,638	. . . .	138,638
Boylston	138,595	. . . .	138,595
Brighton	127,103	7,285	134,388
Charlestown	122,494	5,372	127,866
City Point	144,762	. . . .	144,762
Codman Square	177,839	7,612	185,451
Dorchester	129,879	2,225	132,104
East Boston	176,130	12,689	188,819
Faneuil	138,234	. . . .	138,234

Fellowes Athenaeum	.	.	.	84,258	13,860	98,118
Hyde Park	.	.	.	142,037	1,974	144,011
Jamaica Plain	.	.	.	120,489	6,213	126,702
Jeffries Point	.	.	.	80,460	....	80,460
Kirstein	.	.	.	63,388	....	63,388
Lower Mills	.	.	.	74,990	....	74,990
Mattapan	.	.	.	205,498	....	205,498
Memorial	.	.	.	222,601	374	222,975
Mount Bowdoin	.	.	.	149,341	....	149,341
Mount Pleasant	.	.	.	94,640	....	94,640
Neponset	.	.	.	69,638	....	69,638
North End	.	.	.	142,991	360	143,351
Orient Heights	.	.	.	92,801	....	92,801
Parker Hill	.	.	.	119,139	....	119,139
Phillips Brooks	.	.	.	46,258	....	46,258
Roslindale	.	.	.	155,533	12,029	167,562
Roxbury Crossing	.	.	.	75,062	....	75,062
South Boston	.	.	.	120,750	20,296	141,046
South End	.	.	.	149,798	4,806	154,604
Tyler Street	.	.	.	52,578	....	52,578
Uphams Corner	.	.	.	211,198	201	211,399
West End	.	.	.	190,014	17,989	208,003
West Roxbury	.	.	.	147,884	15,205	163,089
				4,291,433	128,490	4,419,923

These figures are condensed into the following:

Books Lent for Home Use, including Circulation through Schools and Institutions

From Central Library (including Central Library books issued through the branches)	756,018
From Business Branch	18,410
From branches (excluding books received from Central Library) .	4,419,923
Total	5,194,351

COMPARATIVE	1933		1934
Central Library circulation (excluding schools and institutions)			
Direct home use	437,827		395,440
Through branches . . .	86,470		78,118
		524,297	473,558
Business Branch	17,614		18,410
Branch libraries circulation (excluding schools and institutions) . .	4,589,393		4,291,433
Schools and institutions circulation (including books from Central through the Branch system)	416,979		410,950
	5,548,283		5,194,351

Under the inter-library loan system with other libraries the following use of books for the purpose of serious research is shown for two successive years:

	1933	1934
Volumes lent from this Library to other libraries in Massachusetts	2,161	2,041
Lent to libraries outsidt of Massachusetts	353	435
Total	2,514	2,476
Applications refused:		
From libraries in Massachusetts	805	753
From libraries outside of Massachusetts	187	166
Total	992	919

The classified direct circulation of the branches was as follows, for two successive years:

	1933		1934	
	VOLUMES	PERCENTAGE	VOLUMES	PERCENTAGE
Fiction for adults . . .	2,175,120	47.4	2,063,092	48.1
Non-fiction for adults . .	595,749	13.0	588,996	13.7
Juvenile fiction . . .	1,249,371	27.2	1,124,569	26.2
Juvenile non-fiction . .	569,153	12.4	514,776	12.0

At the Central Library the classified direct circulation shows the following percentages:

	1933	1934
	PERCENTAGE	PERCENTAGE
Fiction	45.8	46.1
Non-fiction	54.2	53.9

BOOK ACCESSIONS
BOOKS ACQUIRED BY PURCHASE

	1933		1934	
For the Central Library:				
From City appropriation . . .	7,482		7,327	
From trust funds income . . .	5,267		3,428	
		12,749		10,755
For branches:				
From City appropriation . . .	41,691		48,214	
From trust funds income . . .	2,182		641	
		43,873		48,855
		56,622		59,610

The following statement includes the accessions by purchase combined with books received by gift or otherwise:

	CENTRAL	BRANCHES	TOTAL VOLUMES
Accessions by purchase	10,755	48,855	59,610
Accessions by gift	3,055	564	3,619
Accessions by exchange	15	. . . .	15
Accessions by periodicals bound	1,407	78	1,485
Accessions by newspapers bound	216	. . . .	216
Accessions by serials bound	1,114	. . . .	1,114
Totals	16,562	49,497	66,059

THE CATALOGUE

	1933 VOLS. AND PARTS	TITLES	1934 VOLS. AND PARTS	TITLES
Catalogued (new):				
Central Library Catalogue	24,218	19,679	19,371	16,593
Serials	7,187	. . . .	5,724	. . . .
Branches	41,878	39,502	47,604	44,640
Recatalogued	16,057	13,019	9,230	6,883
Totals	89,340	72,200	81,929	68,116

SHELF DEPARTMENT

The number of volumes shelved and thus made available for public use, taken from the report of the Shelf Department, is:

Placed on the Central Library shelves during the year:
General collection, new books (including continuations) — 15,714
Special collections, new books and transfers — 3,168
Books reported lost or missing in previous years but now found, transfers from branches, etc. — 1,480

20,362

Removed from Central Library shelves during the year:
Books reported lost or missing, condemned copies not yet replaced, transfers, etc. — 3,881

Net gain at Central Library — 16,481
Net gain at Branches — 1,341
Placed in Business Branch — 1,770

Net gain entire library system — 19,592

The total number of volumes available for public use at the end of each year since the formation of the Library is shown in the following statement:

Year	Volumes	Year	Volumes
1852–53	9,688	1894	610,375
1853–54	16,221	1895	628,297
1854–55	22,617	1896–97	663,763
1855–56	28,080	1897–98	698,888
1856–57	34,896	1898–99	716,050
1857–58	70,851	1899–1900.	746,383
1858–59	78,043	1900–01	781,377
1859–60	85,031	1901–02	812,264
1860–61	97,386	1902–03	835,904
1861–62	105,034	1903–04	848,884
1862–63	110,563	1904–05	871,050
1863–64	116,934	1905–06	878,933
1864–65	123,016	1906–07	903,349
1865–66	130,678	1907–08	922,348
1866–67	136,080	1908–09	941,024
1867–68	144,092	1909–10	961,522
1868–69	152,796	1910–11	987,268
1869–70	160,573	1911–12	1,006,717
1870–71	179,250	1912–13	1,049,011
1871–72	192,958	1913–14	1,067,103
1872–73	209,456	1914–15	1,098,702
1873–74	260,550	1915–16	1,121,747
1874–75	276,918	1916–17	1,139,682
1875–76	297,873	1917–18	1,157,326
1876–77	321,010	1918–19	1,173,695
1877–78	345,734	1919–20	1,197,498
1878–79	360,963	1920–21	1,224,510
1879–80	377,225	1921–22	1,258,211
1880–81	390,982	1922–23	1,284,094
1881–82	404,221	1923–24	1,308,041
1882–83	422,116	1924–25	1,333,264
1883–84	438,594	1925	1,363,515
1884–85	453,947	1926	1,388,439
1885	460,993	1927	1,418,489
1886	479,421	1928	1,442,802
1887	492,956	1929	1,475,743
1888	505,872	1930	1,526,951
1889	520,508	1931	1,572,802
1890	536,027	1932	1,631,422
1891	556,283	1933	1,654,017
1892	576,237	1934	1,673,609
1893	597,152		

Volumes in entire library system 1,673,609
Volumes in the Business Branch 15,401
Volumes in the branches 501,560

These volumes are located as follows:

Central Library	. . .	1,156,648	Mattapan	. . .	17,034
Business Branch	. . .	15,401	Memorial	. . .	19,808
Allston	. . .	13,240	Mt. Bowdoin	. . .	13,420
Andrew Square	. . .	11,470	Mt. Pleasant	. . .	8,154
Boylston	. . .	10,844	Neponset	. . .	7,744
Brighton	. . .	22,304	North End	. . .	13,267
Charlestown	. . .	17,051	Orient Heights	. . .	8,772
City Point	. . .	12,148	Parker Hill	. . .	13,096
Codman Square	. . .	16,951	Phillips Brooks	. . .	5,143
Dorchester	. . .	16,889	Roslindale	. . .	15,153
East Boston	. . .	21,607	Roxbury Crossing	. . .	5,840
Faneuil	. . .	12,452	South Boston	. . .	20,845
Fellowes Athenaeum	. . .	40,950	South End	. . .	12,043
Hyde Park	. . .	30,655	Tyler Street	. . .	7,731
Jamaica Plain	. . .	18,858	Uphams Corner	. . .	17,604
Jeffries Point	. . .	8,274	West End	. . .	25,138
Kirstein	. . .	7,803	West Roxbury	. . .	21,419
Lower Mills	. . .	7,853			

THE BINDING DEPARTMENT

	1933	1934
Number of volumes bound in various styles	75,923	69,380
Magazines stitched	103	65
Volumes repaired	1,825	1,549
Volumes guarded	763	702
Photographs and engravings mounted	2,835	2,640
Library publications folded, stitched and trimmed . . .	69,358	82,613

THE PRINTING DEPARTMENT

	1933	1934
Requisitions received and filled	246	215
Card Catalogue (Central Library):		
Titles (Printing Department count)	11,100	17,790
Cards finished (exclusive of "extras")	97,431	133,517
Card Catalogue (Branches):		
Titles (Printing Department count)	704	1,070
Cards finished (exclusive of "extras")	45,760	69,550
Signs	1,478	622
Blank forms (numbered series)	4,102,335	4,184,310
Forms, circulars and sundries (outside the numbered series) .	47,725	44,900
Catalogues, pamphlets, bibliographical programmes . . .	57,200	60,150

OUTSTANDING BOOK PURCHASES

Addison, Joseph. Poems on several occasions. With a dissertation upon
the Roman poets. London. 1719.

Chaucer, Geoffrey. The woorkes of Geffrey Chaucer, newly printed,
with divers addicions, whiche were never in printe before . . .

Colophon (London: Imprinted by John Kyngston for John Wright. 1561).

Davenport, Cyril. Roger Payne, English bookbinder of the eighteenth century. Chicago. Printed for the Caxton Club. 1929.

Donne, John. Letters to severall persons of honour . . . London. Printed by John Flesher, for Richard Marriott. 1651. First edition.

Fay, Bernard. Notes on the American press at the end of the eighteenth Century. Limited edition of 325 copies. New York. The Grolier Club. 1927.

Flavell, John. Husbandry spiritualized: or, The heavenly use of earthly things . . . 10th edition. Boston. Re-printed by John Allen, for Nicholas Boone, at the Sign of the Bible in Cornhill, near the Corner of School-street. 1709.

Fox, Thomas. The Wilmington almanack, or Ephemeris, for the year of our Lord 1775 . . . Wilmington. Printed and sold by James Adams.

Iacovleff, A. and S. Elisseeff. Le théatre japonais (Kabuki). Paris. Jacques de Brunhoff, chez Jules Meynial. n.d.

Lamb, Charles and Mary Lamb. Tales from Shakespear, designed for the use of young persons. London. Printed for Thomas Hodgkins. 1807. 2 vols.

[Milton, John.] The doctrine and discipline of divorce . . . The author, I. M. London. Imprinted in the yeare 1645.

Milton, John. Paradise regain'd: a poem. In IV books. To which is added Samson Agonistes. London. Printed by J. M. for John Starkey at the Mitre in Fleetstreet, near Temple-Bar. 1671.

The New-England Primer improved, for the more easy attaining the true reading of English. To which is added, The assembly of Divines, and Mr. Cotton's catechism. Boston. Printed and sold by Benjamin Edes and Sons. In Cornhill. 1784.

Otway, Thomas. The complete works of . . . Edited by Montague Summers. London. Nonesuch Press. 1926. 3 vols.

Persian manuscripts. Two specimens of Persian writing. Two prayer books in Persian. Persian miniature painting, a page from a book.

Robertson, John W. Bibliography and commentary on the writings of Edgar A. Poe. San Francisco. The Grabhorn Press. 1934. 2 vols.

Roosevelt, Franklin D. Photograph of Cabinet. With autographs of members.

Shelley, Percy Bysshe. Prometheus unbound . . . With other poems. London. 1820. First edition, second issue.

[Tennyson, Alfred.] Poems. By two brothers. London. Printed for W. Simpkin and R. Marshall and J. and J. Jackson. Louth. 1827.

SELECTED LIST OF GIFTS AND GIVERS

Amherst College, Trustees of. The Folger Shakespeare Library, Washington. Published for the Trustees of Amherst College, Amherst, 1933.

Bellows, Mrs. H. P. A collection of sixteen hundred and fifty-six photographs, principally architectural views, landscapes, and reproductions of famous pictures.

Boston Athenaeum. John Adams's Book: being notes on a record of the births, marriages & deaths of three generations of the Adams Family, 1734–1807. Compiled by Henry Adams. Printed for the Boston Athenaeum. 1934. (One of) one hundred and fifty copies printed by D. B. Updike, The Merrymount Press, Boston, in the month of May, 1934.

Brown, Charles S. The Seamans Family in America, as descended from Thomas Seamans of Swansea, Massachusetts, 1687. Compiled by John Julian Lawton, with the . . . financial assistance of Charles Seamans Brown. Privately printed, Syracuse, 1933.

Bull, William P. The Perkins Bull Collection: historical paintings by Canadian artists illustrating pioneers and pioneering in the County of Peel. Printed privately for the founder of the Collection at the Town of Brampton in the County of Peel, (1934?).

De Forest, Col. & Mrs. L. Effingham. Captain John Underhill, Gentleman, Soldier of Fortune. By L. Effingham de Forest and Anne Lawrence de Forest. New York, De Forest Publishing Company, 1934. Designed and printed by the Argus Press as a reprint from: Atterbury and Allied Families. One of an edition of 75 copies.

Gallatin, Albert Eugene. Gallatin iconography. By Albert Eugene Gallatin. Privately printed, 1934. One of an edition of one hundred copies printed by D. B. Updike, The Merrymount Press, Boston, in March, 1934.

Harrison, Fairfax. Early American turf stock, 1780–1830. Being a critical study of the extant evidence for the English, Spanish and Oriental horses and mares, to which are traced the oldest American turf pedigrees. Volume 1: Mares. Privately printed, The Old Dominion Press, Richmond, 1934.

Harrison, Francis Burton. Indo-China: a sportsman's opportunity. By Archibald Harrison. Privately printed, Mayflower Press, Plymouth, 1933. Burton chronicles of colonial Virginia, being excerpts from the existing records particularly relating to the Burtons of the valley of the James and Appomattox, with especial reference to the ancestry of Jesse Burton of Lynchburg (1750?–1795). By Francis Burton Harrison. Privately printed, 1933.

Hispanic Society of America. The visionary gentleman: Don Quijote de la Manche. By Miguel de Cervantes Saavedra. Translated into English by Robinson Smith. Third edition, complete, with a life of Cervantes, notes and appendices. Parts 1 and 2. Printed by order of the Trustees, Hispanic Society of America, New York, 1932. Number 149 of two hundred numbered copies. Urrabieta Vierge and illustrators of Don Quixote (19th and 20th centuries): and exhibition from books in the Library of the Hispanic Society of America. Printed by order of the Trustees, New York, 1934.

Hoff, Madame Whitney. Lettres autographes composant la collection de Madame G. Whitney Hoff. Paris, Cornuau, 1934. "Cet ouvrage á été tiré à 200 exemplaires numérotés, sur papier vélin d'Arches. Exemplaire 88."

Holbrook, Donald. Memorial biography of Walter Hills Holbrook, 1861–1933. The eighth copy (of ten copies printed). Bound in blue leather, with white silk end-pages.

Lane, Mrs. William C. Manuscript letter, dated July 5, 1849, from Helen M. Fiske, to her guardian, Mr. Julius A. Palmer, requesting permission for herself and her sister Annie to board with a Mrs. Clark in Andover, Massachusetts, during a portion of the summer.

Lilly, Josiah K. Foster Hall Reproductions: Songs, compositions and arrangements by Stephen Collins Foster, 1826–1864. Produced by the Staff of Foster Hall. Privately printed by Josiah Kirby Lilly, Indianapolis, 1933. This includes two hundred and twenty-five pieces of music, and one volume of collected music, facsimiles of first (or earliest known) editions of songs by Stephen Collins Foster. Number 713 of 1000 sets.

Marble, Mrs. Arthur De Merrick. Two portfolios, containing one hundred and ten paintings of wild flowers found in Massachusetts and Mississippi, drawn, painted and mounted by Arthur D. Marble.

Massachusetts Public Works of Art Project. Two hundred and sixty-four mounted photographs of the work of artists of the Federal Emergency Relief Administration, Public Works of Art Project, District Number 1, The New England States.

Mediaeval Academy of America. Kodex Quartus Sancti Iacobi de expedimento et conversione Yspanie et Gallecie editus a Beato Turpino Archiepiscopo. One of three hundred copies printed at the Merrymount Press, Boston, for Ward Thoron, May, 1934.

Morris, Lawrence J. The Johnson and allied families of Lincolnshire, England: being the ancestry and posterity of Lawrence Johnson of Philadelphia, Pennsylvania. By Robert Winder Johnson, Sr. (1910) and Lawrence Johnson Morris (1934). Printed for private circulation, Philadelphia, the Dolphin Press, 1934.

Peabody, Francis G. Francis Weld Peabody, 1881–1927: a memoir. Privately printed at the Riverside Press, Cambridge, 1933.

Pforzheimer, Carl H. Surrey's Fourth Boke of Virgill. Edited, with introduction, variant readings and notes by Herbert Hartman. Privately printed for Carl H. Pforzheimer. Printed by John Johnson at the University Press, Oxford. Number 38 of an edition of two hundred and fifty copies, of which one hundred and twenty-five are for private distribution.

Skinner, William. The Belle Skinner Collection of old musical instruments, Holyoke, Massachusetts. A descriptive catalogue compiled under the direction of William Skinner. 1933.

LECTURES — CONCERTS

During 1934 there were given in the Lecture Hall of the Central Library 113 programs under the auspices of the Library. This group of lectures, entertainments, and concerts included a series of 9 concerts given by the E. R. A. Opera Orchestra.

PUBLIC EXHIBITIONS OF 1934

Throughout the year there were on display in the Exhibition Room, Treasure Room, and Children's Room numerous exhibitions assembled from the Library's collections or loaned to the Library by outside sources.

TRUST FUNDS.

Artz Fund — Donation from MISS VICTORINE THOMAS ARTZ, of Chicago: the income of this sum to be employed in the purchase of valuable, rare editions of the writings, either in verse or prose of American and foreign authors. These books are to be known as the "Longfellow Memorial Collection." Received in 1896.
$10,000.00

Bates Fund — Donation made by JOSHUA BATES, of London, in March, 1853.
"The income only of this fund is to be each and every year expended in the purchase of such books of permanent value and authority as may be found most needful and most useful." Payable to the Mayor of the City for the time being. $50,000.00

Charles H. L. N. Bernard Fund — Bequest of CHARLES H. L. N. BER-
NARD. Received in 1930. $2,000.00

Bigelow Fund — Donation made by JOHN P. BIGELOW in August,
1850, when Mayor of the city.
The income from this fund is to be appropriated for the purchase of
books for the increase of the library. $1,000.00

Robert Charles Billings Fund — Bequest of ROBERT CHARLES BIL-
LINGS.
"The sum to constitute a permanent fund for said library, to be
called the Robert Charles Billings Fund, the income only to be used
for the purpose of the purchase of books for said library." Received in 1903. $100,446.10

Bowditch Fund — Bequest of J. INGERSOLL BOWDITCH. Received in
1890.
The whole income in each and every year to be expended in the
purchase of books of permanent value and authority in mathematics
and astronomy. $10,000.00

Bradlee Fund — Bequest of the REV. CALEB DAVIS BRADLEE to the
Boston Public Library. Received in 1897. $1,000.00

Joseph H. Center Fund — Bequest of JOSEPH H. CENTER, the income
thereof to be at all times applied to the purchase of books and other
additions to the library. Received in 1905. $39,908.89

Children's Fund — Bequest of JOSIAH H. BENTON of $100,000, to be
held as "The Children's Fund," and the income applied to the purchase of books for the use of the young, to be applied for those purposes only in years when the city appropriates for the maintenance
of the Library at least three per cent of the amount available for
department expenses from taxes and income in said city. In any year
when the city does not thus appropriate at least three per cent of the
amount available for department expenses from taxes and income in
said City, the income given in said will for the purchase of books
shall be paid to the Rector of Trinity Church in the City of Boston
to be by him dispensed in relieving the necessities of the poor.
                                                          $107,060.53

Clement Fund — Bequest of the late FRANK CLEMENT, of Newton, to
be known as the "Frank Clement Fund," the income to be applied
to the purchase of books. Received in 1915. $2,000.00

Henry Sargent Codman Memorial Fund — This is a contribution from
the friends of HENRY SARGENT CODMAN, to be used to perpetuate
the memory of Mr. Codman by the purchase of books upon land-
scape gardening. It is the desire of the subscribers that a special

book plate shall be inserted in each of the volumes purchased, identifying it as part of their memorial collection. Received in 1898.

$2,854.41

Cutter Fund — Bequest of ABRAM E. CUTTER of four thousand dollars and his library of books, the income of the fund to be expended for the purchase of books, and for binding. Received in 1901.

$4,270.00

Elizabeth Fund — Bequest of SARAH A. MATCHETT, late of Brookline, who died October 6, 1910, the object of which is stated in the following extract from her will:

"I give and bequeath to the Trustees of the Public Library of the City of Boston, twenty-five thousand dollars, to be called the Elizabeth fund, to be received, held and securely invested, and only the net income therefrom expended every year in the purchase of such books of permanent value and authority as may be most useful in said Library." $25,000.00

Daniel Sharp Ford Fund — A bequest of DANIEL SHARP FORD to the Public Library of the City of Boston, to be used for the purchase of books for the young until otherwise ordered by the Board. Received in 1900. $6,000.00

Franklin Club Fund — Donation made in June, 1863, by a literary association of young men in Boston, who, at the dissolution of the association, authorized its trustees, Thomas Minns, John J. French and J. Franklin Reed, to dispose of the funds on hand in such manner as to them should seem judicious. They elected to bestow them on the Public Library, attaching thereto only the following conditions: "In trust, that the income, but the income only, shall, year by year, be expended in the purchase of books of permanent value, for the use of the free Public Library of the city, and as far as practicable of such a character as to be of special interest to young men." The trustees expressed a preference for books relative to government and political economy. $1,000.00

Isabella Stewart Gardner Fund — Bequest of ISABELLA STEWART GARDNER.

"To the Trustees of the Boston Public Library, for the Brown Musical Library, for a memorial to B. J. Lang." Received in 1924. $5,000.00

Morris Gest Fund — Donation made by MR. MORRIS GEST in December 1925, the gross receipts from a benefit performance for the Library of "The Miracle", — $2,652.50, the income to be used in the interest of dramatic art. $2,652.50

Green Fund — Donations of Dr. Samuel A. Green of $2,000, the income of which is to be expended for the purchase of books relating to American history.   Received in 1878 and 1884.   **$2,000.00**

Charlotte Harris Fund — Bequest of Charlotte Harris, late of Boston, the object of which is stated in the following extract from her will: "I give to the Charlestown Public Library $10,000, to be invested on interest, which interest is to be applied to the purchase of books published before 1850. I also give to said Public Library my own private library and the portrait of my grandfather, Richard Devens." Bequests accepted by City Council, July 31, 1877.
$10,000.00

Thomas B. Harris Fund — Bequest of Thomas B. Harris, late of Charlestown, for the benefit of the Charlestown Public Library. Received in 1884.   **$1,048.93**

Alfred Hemenway Fund — Bequest of Alfred Hemenway. Received in 1928.   **$5,000.00**

Hyde Fund — Bequest of Franklin P. Hyde of Boston, to be known as the "Franklin P. Hyde Fund," the income to be applied to the purchase of books and other library material.   Received in 1915.
$3,632.40

David P. Kimball Fund — Bequest of David P. Kimball. "I give to the Public Library of the City of Boston, the income to be used for the purchase of books, $10,000." Received in 1924.
$10,271.58

Louis E. Kirstein Fund — Donations of $1,000 each made by Mr. Louis E. Kirstein, "to be used for any purpose of the Library that the Trustees see fit to put it to."

October, 1925 .	$1,000.00
October, 1926 .	1,000.00
November, 1927	1,000.00
October, 1928 .	1,000.00
October, 1929 .	1,000.00
	$5,000.00

Arthur Mason Knapp Fund — Extract from the will of Katherine Knapp: "To the Trustees of the Public Library of the City of Boston, the sum of ten thousand dollars ($10,000), to be known as the Arthur Mason Knapp Fund, of which the income only shall be used for the purchase of books for said library. And I hereby request that such books be designated with an appropriate label or inscription, bearing the name of the Fund." Received in 1914.

$10,002.50

Helen Lambert Fund — Bequest of Helen Lambert of Boston in memory of Frederic and Louise Lambert. Received in 1931. The income of this fund to be expended for the purchase of books and other library material until otherwise ordered by the Board. $1,371.00

Abbott Lawrence Fund — Bequest of ABBOTT LAWRENCE, of Boston. Received in 1860. The interest on this fund is to be exclusively appropriated for the purchase of books for the said library having a permanent value. $10,000.00

Edward Lawrence Fund — Bequest of EDWARD LAWRENCE, of Charlestown. Received in 1886. The following clause from his will explains its purpose:

"To hold and apply the income and so much of the principal as they may choose, to the purchase of special books of reference to be kept and used only at the Charlestown branch of said Public Library."

500.00

Mrs. John A. Lewis Fund — Bequest of ELIZABETH LEWIS, to be known as the Mrs. John A. Lewis Fund: "I give and bequeath to the Boston Public Library the sum of $5,000 as a fund, the income of which is to be used for the purchase of such old and rare books as shall be fitly selected to augment the collection known as the John A. Lewis Library." Received in 1903. $5,000.00

Charles Greely Loring Memorial Fund — Donation from the family of CHARLES GREELY LORING, the income of which is to be expended for the purchase of books for the West End Branch. Received in 1896. $500.00

Charles Mead Fund — Bequest of CHARLES MEAD, to constitute the Charles Mead Public Library Trust Fund for the promotion of the objects of the Public Library in such manner as the government of said library shall deem best, and so far as the government shall deem consistent with the objects of the library to be used for the benefit of the South Boston Branch Library. Received in 1896.

$2,530.51

Gardner O. North Fund — Bequest of Gardner O. North. Received in 1928. $2,000.00

The Oakland Hall Trust Fund — By an interlocutory decree of the Probate Court for the County of Suffolk, the amount of $11,781.44 was received, the same being one-half of the net amount received from the disposition of certain property held by the Trustees, under an indenture between Amor Hollingsworth, Sumner A. Burt and Amor L. Hollingsworth, all of Milton, Mass., and John H. Mc-Kendry, of Boston, Mass., entered into the sixth day of August, 1870. The above amount was accepted by the City, January 2, 1924, and the Trustees of the Public Library voted to invest the same under the name of "The Oakland Hall Trust Fund," the income to be applied to the purchase of books and other library material for the Mattapan Branch. $11,781.44

John Boyle O'Reilly Fund — Donation received from the PAPYRUS CLUB to establish a fund in memory of John Boyle O'Reilly, late member of said club, the income of said fund to be devoted to the purchase of books for the Boston Public Library. Received in 1897.
$1,085.02

Phillips Fund — Donation made by JONATHAN PHILLIPS, of Boston, in April, 1853.
The interest of this fund is to be used exclusively for the purchase of books for said library. $10,000.00
Also a bequest by the same gentleman in his will dated September 20, 1849.
The interest on which is to be annually devoted to the maintenance of a free Public Library. $20,000.00
Both of these items are payable to the Mayor of the City for the time being.

Pierce Fund — Donation made by HENRY L. PIERCE, Mayor of the City, November 29, 1873, and accepted by the City Council, December 27, 1873. $5,000.00

Sarah E. Pratt Fund — Bequest from SARAH E. PRATT, late of Boston, under the 14th clause of her will, for the benefit of the Dorchester Branch, $500.00. Received in January, 1922. Distribution of residue of estate in May, 1924, $964.30. $1,494.18

Guilford Reed Fund — Bequest of Helen Leah Reed, as a memorial to Guilford S. Reed; the income to be applied to the purchase of books of non-fiction. $1,000.00

John Singer Sargent Fund — Balance remaining in hands of surviving trustees of fund originally raised to install in the Library decorations by John Singer Sargent; the income to be used for the care and preservation of the Sargent decorations, etc. $3,858.24

Scholfield Fund — Bequest of ARTHUR SCHOLFIELD, who died in New York, January 17, 1883. The interest to be paid to certain heirs during their lives, and then to be used for the purchase of books of permanent value. The last heir, Joseph Scholfield, died November 18, 1889, and by his will bequeathed to the City of Boston the sum of $11,766.67, which represents the income of said fund received by him up to the time of his death, to which was added $33.33 accrued interest on deposit up to the time of investment, to be added to the fund given by his brother. $62,242.45

Sewall Fund — Extract from the will of RICHARD BLACK SEWALL: "*Tenth.* — I bequeath the following pecuniary legacies clear of legacy tax, namely, To the Trustees of the Public Library of the City of Boston $25,000 to be added to their funds and the income to be used for the purchase of books." Received in 1918.
$25,000.00

Skinner Fund — Extract from the will of FRANCIS SKINNER: "*Eleventh.* — All my books and library I give and bequeath to my son, to be enjoyed by him during his life and after his death to be distributed as he shall appoint among such public libraries, as he shall judge fit, and in case he makes no such appointment then to the Trustees of the Public Library of the City of Boston.
"*Sixteenth.* — All the rest and residue of my said property of whatever kind, I give and bequeath to Augustus P. Loring and J. Lewis Stackpole in trust to pay the net income to my son Francis Skinner, Jr., during his life, or to apply the same to his maintenance and support, or the maintenance and support of any issue of his, as they shall think best during his life; and at his death to apply the income to the maintenance and support of his issue until his youngest child shall reach the age of 21 years and then to distribute said property among said issue, the issue of a deceased child to take the share a parent would have if living.
"If there shall be no issue surviving at the time of my son's death, then to turn the said property into cash and to divide it equally among the following legatees: The Trustees of the Public Library of the City of Boston, the Museum of Fine Arts of Boston, Massachusetts, the Massachusetts General Hospital, the Medical School of Harvard University, and the Free Hospital for Women, Brookline, Massachusetts." Received in 1914. $51,732.14

South Boston Branch Library Trust Fund — Donation of a citizen of South Boston, the income of which is to be expended for the benefit of the South Boston Branch Library. Received in 1879.
$100.00

Mary Elizabeth Stewart Fund — Bequest of MARY ELIZABETH STEWART of $3,500 to the Trustees of the Boston Public Library. The

Trustees voted under date of June 29, 1923, that the income be
applied to the purchase of books and other library material.

$3,500.00

James Jackson Storrow (Harvard '57) Fund — Gift of Helen Storrow
and Elizabeth Randolph Storrow as a memorial to James Jackson
Storrow, Senior; income to be used for the purchase of Italian books.

$25,000.00

Patrick F. Sullivan Bequest — Extract from will: "I give and bequeath
to the Trustees of the Boston Public Library the sum of five thous-
and dollars, the principal or income of said sum to be expended by
them for the purchase of Catholic standard books, said books to be
approved by the Archbishop of the diocese of Boston, Mass., or by
the President of the Trustees of Boston College, in Boston, Mass."
Received in 1908.

This bequest, together with interest amounting to $339.61, has been
expended for books.

Ticknor Bequest — By the will of GEORGE TICKNOR, of Boston, he
gave to the City of Boston, on the death of his wife, all his books
and manuscripts in the Spanish and Portuguese languages, about
four thousand volumes, and also the sum of four thousand dollars.
After the receipt of said sums the city is required to spend not less
than one thousand dollars in every five years during the twenty-five
years next succeeding (i.e., the income of four thousand dollars, at
the rate of five per cent per annum) in the purchase of books in the
Spanish and Portuguese languages and literature. At the end of
twenty-five years the income of said sum to be expended annually in
the purchase of books of permanent value, either in the Spanish or
Portuguese languages, or in such other languages as may be deemed
expedient by those having charge of the library. The books bequeathed or purchased are always to be freely accessible for reference or study, but are not to be loaned for use outside of the library
building. If these bequests are not accepted by the city, and the
trusts and conditions faithfully executed, the books, manuscripts and
money are to be given to the President and Fellows of Harvard
College. In order that the city might receive the immediate benefit
of this contribution, Anna Ticknor, widow of the donor, relinquished
her right to retain during her life the books and manuscripts, and
placed them under the control of the city, the City Council having
previously accepted the bequests in accordance with the terms and

conditions of said will, and the Trustees of the Public Library received' said bequests on behalf of the city, and made suitable arrangements for the care and custody of the books and manuscripts. Received in 1871. $4,106.71

William C. Todd Newspaper Fund — Donation by WILLIAM C. TODD, accepted by order of the City Council, approved October 30, 1897, the income to be at least two thousand dollars a year, to be expended by the Library Trustees for newspapers of this and other countries. $50,000.00

Townsend Fund— Donation from William Minot and William Minot, Jr., executors of the will of MARY P. TOWNSEND, of Boston, at whose disposal she left a certain portion of her estate in trust for such charitable and public institutions as they might think meritorious. Said executors accordingly selected the Public Library of the City of Boston as one of such institutions, and attached the following conditions to the legacy: "The income only shall, in each and every year, be expended in the purchase of books for the use of the library; each of which books shall have been published in some one edition at least five years at the time it may be so purchased." Received in 1879. $4,000.00

Treadwell Fund — By the will of the late DANIEL TREADWELL, of Cambridge, late Rumford Professor in Harvard College, who died February 27, 1872, he left the residue of his estate, after payment of debts, legacies, etc., in trust to his executors, to hold during the life of his wife for her benefit, and after her decease to divide the residue then remaining in the hands of the Trustees, as therein provided, and convey one-fifth part thereof to the Trustees of the Public Library of the City of Boston.
By order of the City Council, approved May 17, 1872, said beuqest was accepted and the Trustees of the Public Library authorized to receive the same and invest it in the City of Boston Bonds, income of which is to be expended by said Trustees in such manner as they may deem for the best interests of the Library. $13,987.69

Tufts Fund — Bequest of NATHAN A. TUFTS, of Charlestown, to be known as the "Nathan A. Tufts Fund," the income to be applied at all times to the purchase of books and other additions to the library to be placed in the Charlestown Branch. Received in 1906. $10,736.68

Twentieth Regiment Memorial Fund — Donation on account of the TWENTIETH REGIMENT MEMORIAL FUND, the income to be used for the purchase of books of a military and patriotic character, to be placed in the alcove appropriated as a memorial to the Twentieth Regiment. Received in 1897. $5,000.00

Horace G. Wadlin Fund — Bequest of HORACE G. WADLIN, of Reading, former Librarian, who died November 5, 1925, of $2,000 to the Trustees of the Public Library of the City of Boston to be permanently funded and the income thereof used for the purchase of books. Received in 1932. $2,030.51

Wales Fund — Extract from the will of GEORGE C. WALES: "After the foregoing bequests I direct that the sum of five thousand dollars be paid to the Trustees of the Public Library of the City of Boston, the same to be held, managed and invested by them, so as to produce an income, and the said income to be applied to the purchase of such books for said Library as they may deem best." Received in 1918. $5,000.00

Mehitable C. C. Wilson Fund. — Bequest of MEHITABLE C. C. WILSON, the income to be expended for the purchase of books for the Boston Public Library. Received in 1913. $1,000.00

Whitney Funds — Bequests of JAMES LYMAN WHITNEY, who died September 25, 1910.

Alice Lincoln Whitney Fund — The twelfth clause of his will directed that: One-tenth of said remaining income of the principal fund, I direct to be paid to the Trustees of the Public Library of the City of Boston, to be held and accumulated by said Trustees and permanently invested and re-invested. The first five thousand dollars of income so accumulated, including the income thereon arising during the period of accumulation, I request to be funded in the name of my sister, Alice Lincoln Whitney, and the income of said fund after its accumulation or so much of said income as may be required, to be paid to such employees of the said Library, who are sick and in need of help, as the Trustees may in their discretion deem most worthy (there are often such cases). Any amount of income from said accumulated fund not needed for the purpose just mentioned shall be used for the purchase of books and manuscripts. $5,000.00

James Lyman Whitney Fund — The Alice Lincoln Whitney Fund having been established, all amounts of income of the principal fund paid to said Trustees, after the accumulation of said fund of five thousand dollars shall be held as the James Lyman Whitney Fund, and invested and re-invested and the income used in equal shares, one share for the purchase of rare and expensive books, and one share

for the purchase and care of manuscripts; one half at least of the
share devoted to manuscripts to be expended for their cataloguing
and proper care. $25,084.37

In addition to the above Mr. Whitney created a trust, directing that
of the net income seven hundred dollars a year be paid to the Trustees of the Public Library of the City of Boston, to be expended on
bibliographic work for the benefit of the Library.

Central Library Building Fund — Donations in response to an appeal by
the Trustees in April, 1925, setting forth the needs of the Library,
from:

Percy Lee Atherton	$ 25.00
William York Peters	25.00
John T. Spaulding	100.00
	$150.00

Donations — Besides the preceding, the following donations have been
made to the Public Library, and the amounts have been appropriated for the purchase of books, according to the intention of the
donors, *viz.*:

Samuel Appleton, late of Boston . . .	$6,800.00
H. C. Bentley	220.38
J. Ingersoll Bowditch	6,800.00
Nathaniel I. Bowditch	200.00
James Brown, late of Cambridge . . .	500.00
Andrew Carnegie	980.75
Dorchester and Milton Circulating Library, for the benefit of the Dorchester Branch Library .	335.13
Sally Inman Kast Shepard	1,000.00
James Nightingale	100.00
	$11,136.26

RECAPITULATION OF PUBLIC LIBRARY TRUST FUNDS.

Artz Fund	$ 10,000.00
Bates Fund	50,000.00
Charles H. L. N. Bernard Fund	2,000.00
Bigelow Fund	1,000.00
Robert Charles Billings Fund	100,482.98
Bowditch Fund	10,000.00
Bradlee Fund	1,000.00
Joseph H. Center Fund	39,908.89
Carried forward	$213,391.87

Brought forward	$213,391.87
Central Library Building Fund	150.00
Children's Fund	107,073.40
Clement Fund	2,000.00
Henry Sargent Codman Memorial Fund	2,854.41
Cutter Fund	4,270.00
Elizabeth Fund	25,000.00
Daniel Sharp Ford Fund	6,000.00
Franklin Club Fund	1,000.00
Isabella Stewart Gardner Fund	5,000.00
Morris Gest Fund	2,652.50
Green Fund	2,000.00
Charlotte Harris Fund	10,000.00
Thomas B. Harris Fund	1,048.93
Alfred Hemenway Fund	5.000.00
Hyde Fund	3,632.40
David P. Kimball Fund	10,236.69
Louis E. Kirstein Fund	5,000.00
Arthur Mason Knapp Fund	10,000.00
Helen Lamber Fund	1,301.00
Abbott Lawrence Fund	10,000.00
Edward Lawrence Fund	500.00
Mrs. John A. Lewis Fund	5,000.00
Charles Greely Loring Memorial Fund	500.00
Charles Mead Fund	2,530.51
Gardner. O. North Fund	2,000.00
The Oakland Hall Trust Fund	11,781.44
John Boyle O'Reilly Fund	1,085.02
Phillips Fund	30,000.00
Pierce Fund	5,000.00
Sarah E. Pratt Fund	1,494.18
Guilford Reed Fund	1,000.00
John Singer Sargent Fund	3,858.24
Scholfield Fund	62,242.45
Sewall Fund	25,000.00
Skinner Fund	51,732.14
South Boston Branch Library Trust Fund	100.00
Mary Elizabeth Stewart Fund	3,500.00
James Jackson Storrow (Harvard '57) Fund	25,000.00
Ticknor Fund	4,106.71
William C. Todd Newspaper Fund	50,000.00
Townsend Fund	4,000.00
Treadwell Fund	13,987.69
Nathan A. Tufts Fund	10,736.68
Twentieth Regiment Memorial Fund	5,000.00
Horace G. Wadlin Fund	2,030.51
Wales Fund	5,000.00
Alice Lincoln Whitney Fund	5,000.00
James Lyman Whitney Fund	25,084.37
Mehitable C. C. Wilson Fund	1,000.00

[49]

OFFICERS OF THE LIBRARY

Director's Office

Director, and Librarian	Milton E. Lord
Clerk of the Trustees	Elizabeth B. Brockunier
Supervisor of Training	Bertha V. Hartzell
Editor of Publications	Zoltán Haraszti

Reference Division

Acting Chief Librarian of the Reference Division: Richard G. Hensley

Assistant Librarian, Emeritus	Frank C. Blaisdell
Assistant Librarian, Emeritus	Otto Fleischner
Assistant Librarian	Pierce E. Buckley
Assistant Librarian	Samuel A. Chevalier

Book Selection Department: Louis F. Ranlett, Chief.
Cataloging and Classification Department: Samuel A. Chevalier, Chief.

General Reference Departments: Pierce E. Buckley, Supervisor.
    Bates Hall Reference Department: Harry W. Mathews, Assistant in Charge.
    Information Department: John H. Reardon, Assistant in Charge.
    Newspaper Department: Frederic Serex, Assistant in Charge.
    Periodical Department: Dorothy P. Shaw, In Charge.
    Registration Department: A. Frances Rogers, Chief.
    Issue Department: Thomas F. Brennan, Chief.

Special Reference Departments: Francis J. Hannigan, Supervisor.
    Special Libraries: George S. Maynard, Chief.
    Fine Arts Department: Mildred R. Bradbury, Assistant in Charge.
    Music Department: Richard G. Appel, Assistant in Charge.
    Genealogy Department: Agnes C. Doyle, Assistant in Charge.
    Patent Department: William J. Ennis, Assistant in Charge.
    Statistical Department: Elizabeth G. Barry, Assistant in Charge.
    Teachers' Department: Anna L. Manning, Assistant in Charge.
    Business Branch: Mary W. Dietrichson, Business Branch Librarian.

Rare Books: Zoltán Haraszti, Keeper of Rare Books.
    Rare Book Department: Harriet Swift, Assistant in Charge.

Circulation Division

Chief Librarian of the Circulation Division: Orlando C. Davis.

Book Selection Department: Louis F. Ranlett, Chief.

Children's Work: Alice M. Jordan, Supervisor.

Branch Libraries: Edith Guerrier, Supervisor.
Branch Librarians:
    Allston, Katherine F. Muldoon.
    Andrew Square, Elizabeth H. McShane.
    Boylston, Margaret A. Calnan.
    Brighton, Katrina M. Sather.
    Charlestown, Katherine S. Rogan.
    City Point, Helen L. Morrisey.
    Codman Square, Elizabeth P. Ross.
    Dorchester, Marion C. Kingman.
    East Boston, Theodora B. Scoff.
    Faneuil, Gertrude L. Connell.
    Fellowes Athenaeum, Mary E. Ames.
    Hyde Park, Sara A. Lyon.
    Jamaica Plain, Katie F. Albert.
    Jeffries Point, Mary U. Nichols, Assistant in Charge.
    Kirstein, Grace B. Loughlin.
    Lower Mills, Isabel E. Wetherald.
    Mattapan, Ada Aserkoff.
    Memorial, Beatrice M. Flanagan.
    Mount Bowdoin, Pearl B. Smart.
    Mount Pleasant, Margaret H. Reid.
    Neponset, Margaret I. McGovern.
    North End, Mary F. Curley.
    Orient Heights, Catherine E. Flannery.
    Parker Hill, Mary M. Sullivan.
    Phillips Brooks, Edna G. Peck.
    Roslindale, Annie M. Donovan.
    Roxbury Crossing, Edith R. Nickerson.
    South Boston, M. Florence Cufflin.
    South End, Clara L. Maxwell.
    Tyler Street, Caroline Keene, Acting Librarian.
    Uphams Corner, Beatrice C. Maguire.
    West End, Fanny Goldstein.
    West Roxbury, Geneva Watson, Assistant in Charge.
Branch Librarian, Emeritus, Carrie L. Morse.

Division of Business Operations

Acting Comptroller: James W. Kenney.

Superintendent of Buildings: William F. Quinn.

Auditor: Helen Schubarth.
Book Purchasing Department: William C. Maiers, Jr., Chief.
Stock Purchasing Department: Timothy J. Mackin.
Binding Department: James P. Mooers, In Charge.
Shipper: Robert F. Dixon.
Printing Department: Francis W. Lee, Chief.

CPSIA information can be obtained
at www.ICGtesting.com
Printed in the USA
BVHW042007101118
532427BV00034B/547/P

9 780483 788213